A "Grammy's Gang" Book
# No Way to Haircut Day!

Written by Flo Barnett
Illustrated by Derek Bacon

No Way to Haircut Day!
Copyright © 2012 by Flo Barnett
All rights reserved. No part of this book may be used or reproduced in any manner whatsoever without written permission except in the case of brief quotations embodied in critical articles and reviews.

Illustrated by Derek Bacon

For more information:
http://www.grammysgang.com
flo.grammysgang@gmail.com

For my wildly cool grandson, Kaden
Love you more!

Why do I need my hair cut?
I'd really like to know.
Why not let my hair grow
down to my tippy toes?

But every month or two
it's haircut day once more,
so me and mom and dad
burst through the barber's door.

The barber smiles at me,
says, "How are you today?
Just hop right in this chair,
my boy, it's haircut day."

I do not move at all.
I give an angry stare.
I will not hop right up
into that barber's chair.

"No way to haircut day!
No way! No way!" I shout.
"I like my hair like this,
so pleeeease don't cut it out!"

Mom says that I'll be fine.
Dad puts me in the seat.
I start to scream and yell
and wildly kick my feet.

"Sit still," the barber says.
"You cannot squirm and jerk.
Jumping about like that,
believe me, just won't work."

But side to side I turn
and twist my head full speed,
'cause if I don't sit still
he'll never do the deed!

The barber's face turns red,
his patience growing thin.
He might give up the fight,
and, in the end, I'll win.

Oh no,
**by gosh**

# BOo-HoO!

It's a BIRD
It's a PLANE!

Dad leaps in front of me
and lifts me in the air.
He puts me on his lap.
Now we both sit in the chair.

Mom holds my head real still
so I can't shift or sway.
Tears trickle down my cheeks
as the barber clips away.

First, hairs on top are cut.
Next, sides and back must go.
"My son, relax, be brave,
a few more hairs or so."

The razor's growl is loud,
so loud it makes me shake,
and as it buzzes louder,
the longer it will take.

At last, the haircut's done!
I cry the biggest sigh

and jump out of the chair
and wonder why, oh, why?

Then looking in the mirror,
a handsome face I see

And much to my surprise…

that handsome face is . . . ME!

The moment comes at last,
the one I've waited for.
I grab a big, red lollipop
and race right out the door.

"Soon you'll sit alone, my son,"
Dad smiles and winks at me.
"You'll be so very proud
next haircut day, you'll see!"

## Coming September 2013!

*When Grammy Goes Away* is the sixth book in the Grammy's Gang series. When a loved one passes, children need to be encouraged to talk about their loss, their feelings, and techniques that they can employ to help them cope. Using humor under such dire circumstances can greatly facilitate these discussions.

*No Way to Haircut Day!, Dirty Face Liam, Calling All Grammies, There's a Baby in Mommy's Belly!, Sweet, Sweet, Sweet Barefeet!* are available as Kindle eBooks as well as in paperback at Amazon.com.

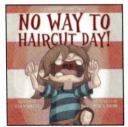 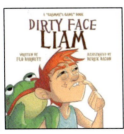 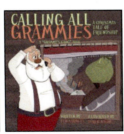  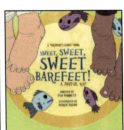

www.grammysgang.com
flo.grammysgang@gmail.com

**Looking for an exciting adventure? Check out The Adventures of Jocker & Bivy by T.J. Hawk!**

Jocker and Bivy are ordinary cardinals, hoping to learn how to fly. But when they learn that their home is in danger from an army of ants, they must take action. With the help of a few new friends they meet along the way, Jocker and Bivy embark on a quest: Saving Upworld!

**If you like Roald Dahl, Judy Blume, or Beverly Cleary, you'll love** *The Adventures of Jocker & Bivy*!

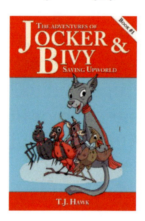

# www.jockerandbivy.com

## About the Author

During her professional career, Flo Barnett was a preschool administrator and daycare provider. She also taught kindergarten and elementary school for many years. Now retired, Flo writes hilarious tales for, and sometimes based on, the real-life antics of her six energetic grandchildren whom she lovingly refers to as "Grammy's Gang." Flo lives near Pittsburgh, Pennsylvania with her hubby, Barry, and her dog, Shadow.

Made in the USA  
Lexington, KY  
21 March 2019